Menzone Drive Tab

Copyright © 2019 Silver Pencil Press. All rights reserved.

No part of this book may be used or reproduced in any manner whatsoever without permission except in the case of brief quotations embodied in critical articles and reviews. For more information, email all inquiries to info@silverpencilpress.com.

Layout and design by Silver Pencil Press
Photography by Curtis Cleaves
Tab|Edit by Lee Marcus

All songs composed and arranged by Dan Menzone except Nerissa which is composed by Peggy Harvey and used with permission and Dear Old Dixie which is composed by L. Flatt & E. Scruggs and used with permission.

Published by Silver Pencil Press, Charlton, MA.

Printed in the United States of America
ISBN-13: 978-1-951016-10-4
Library of Congress Control Number: 2019917366

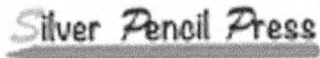

Menzone Drive Tab

Song Title	Key	Page
Menzone Drive	A, Capo 2	1
Restless	G	14
Clara's Reel	C	25
2720	A, Capo 2	37
Deck Speed	D	45
Dear Old Dixie	G	54
Joe and Evelyn	C	66
Rooster's Rag	G	72
Nerissa	Am, Capo 2	81
Stone Bench	Gm	85

Dan has had a long, industrious career playing the 5-String Banjo, including eighteen years the New England based bluegrass band Traver Hollow. The CD featuring these songs, "Menzone Drive," was Dan's first solo project, released in 2006 and his first partnering with Wyatt Rice on guitar. Wyatt and Dan have since produced and recorded additional projects, including the 2009 CD "Frostbite" and the 2015 CD "Something out of the Blue" both of which feature some of Dan's phenomenal, well-written, banjo tunes.

Thank you for supporting bluegrass music, the 5-String Banjo, and Dan!

Menzone Drive

Key of A, Capo 2

Menzone Drive
Page 4/13

Menzone Drive

Menzone Drive
Page 10/13

Menzone Drive
Page 11/13

Menzone Drive
Page 12/13

Menzone Drive
Page 13/13

Restless

Key of G

Restless
Page 2/11

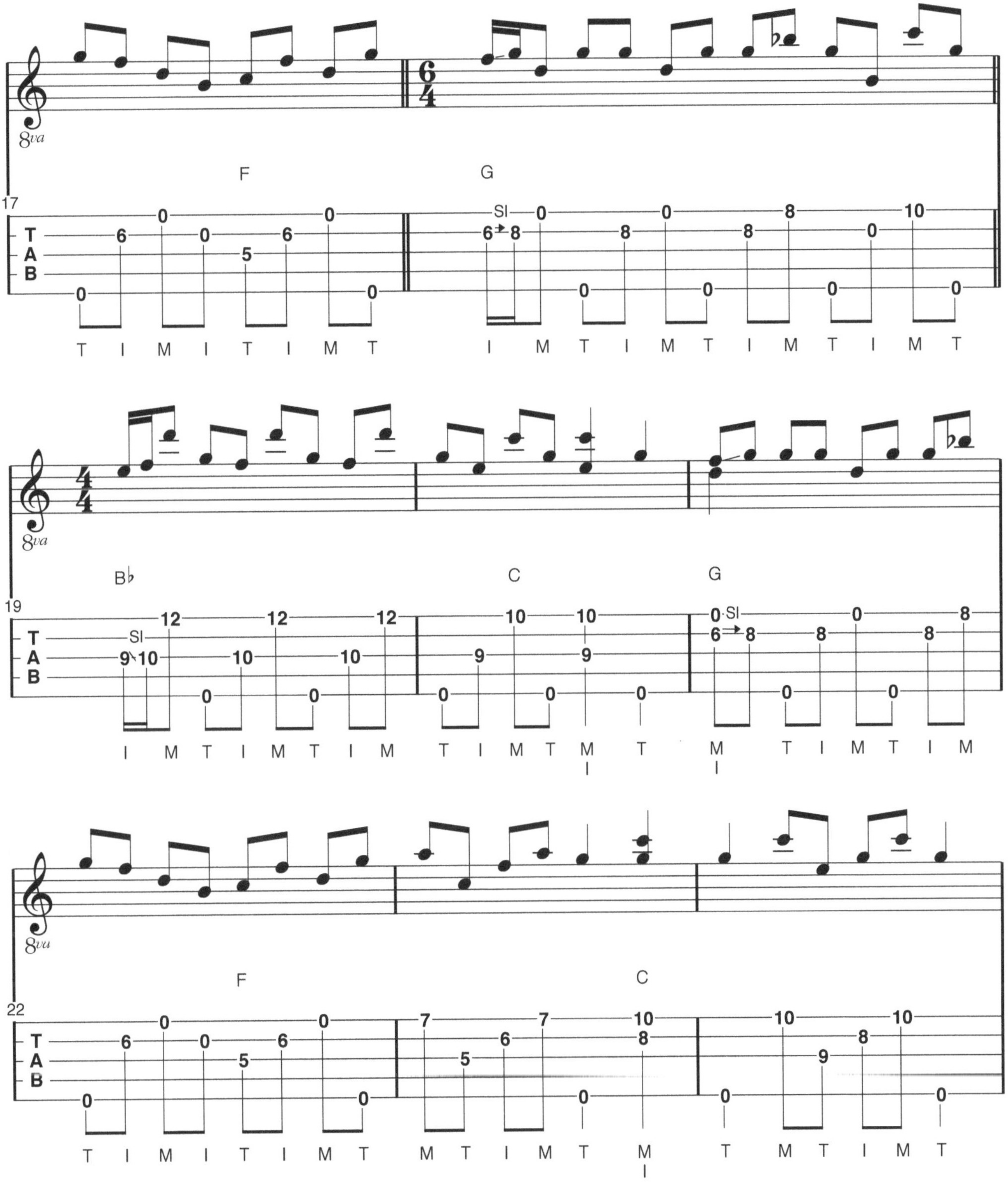

Restless
Page 4/11

17

Restless
Page 5/11

Restless

Restless
Page 8/11

21

Restless
Page 10/11

23

Restless
Page 11/11

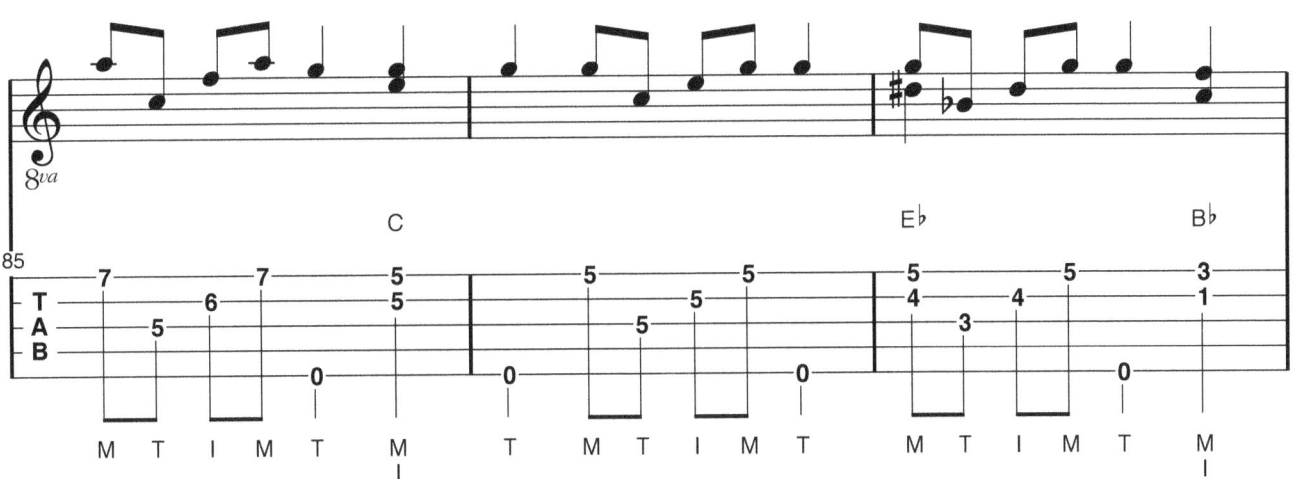

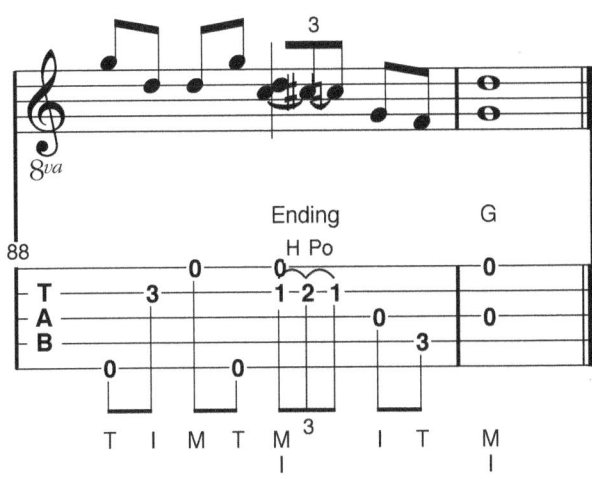

24

Clara's Reel

Key of C
Page 1/12

Clara's Reel
Page 2/12

Clara's Reel
Page 3/12

27

Clara's Reel
Page 5/12

Clara's Reel
Page 6/12

Clara's Reel
Page 9/12

33

Clara's Reel
Page 10/12

34

Clara's Reel
Page 11/12

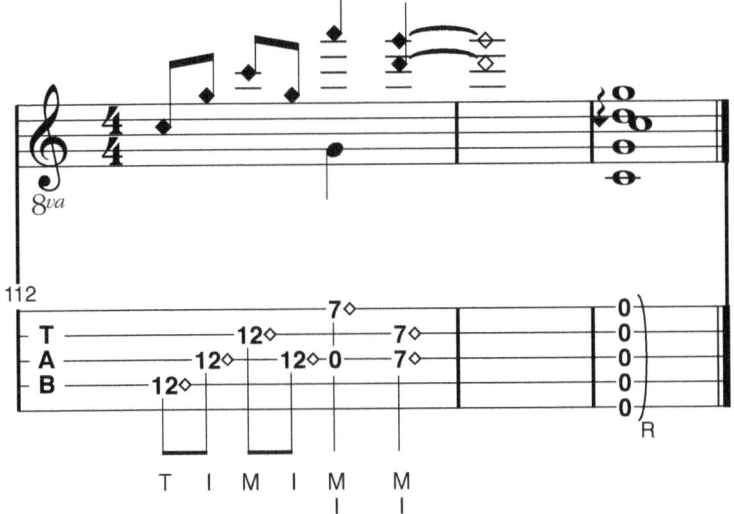

2720

Key of A, Capo 2
Page 1/8

Deck Speed

Key of D
Page 1/9

Deck Speed
Page 2/9

Deck Speed
Page 3/9

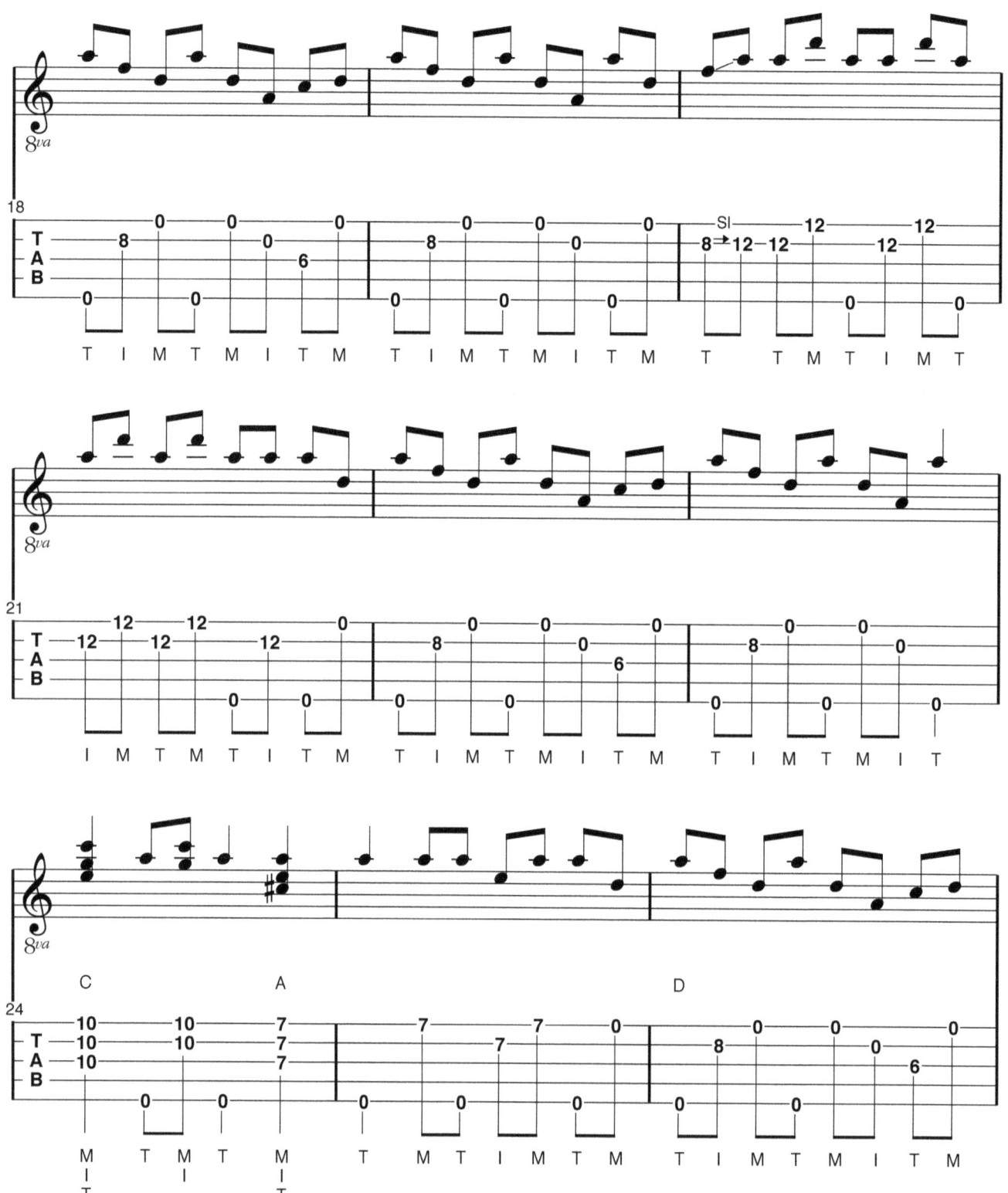

Deck Speed
Page 5/9

Deck Speed
Page 6/9

50

Deck Speed
Page 7/9

Deck Speed
Page 8/9

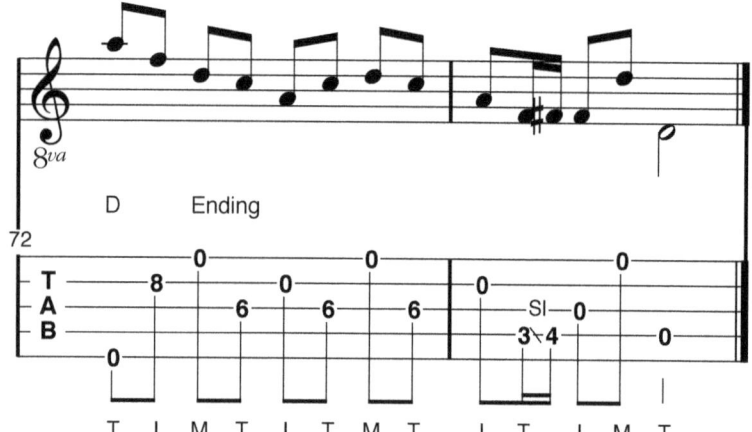

Dear Old Dixie

Key of G
Page 1/12

Dear Old Dixie
Page 2/12

Dear Old Dixie
Page 3/12

Dear Old Dixie
Page 4/12

Dear Old Dixie
Page 5/12

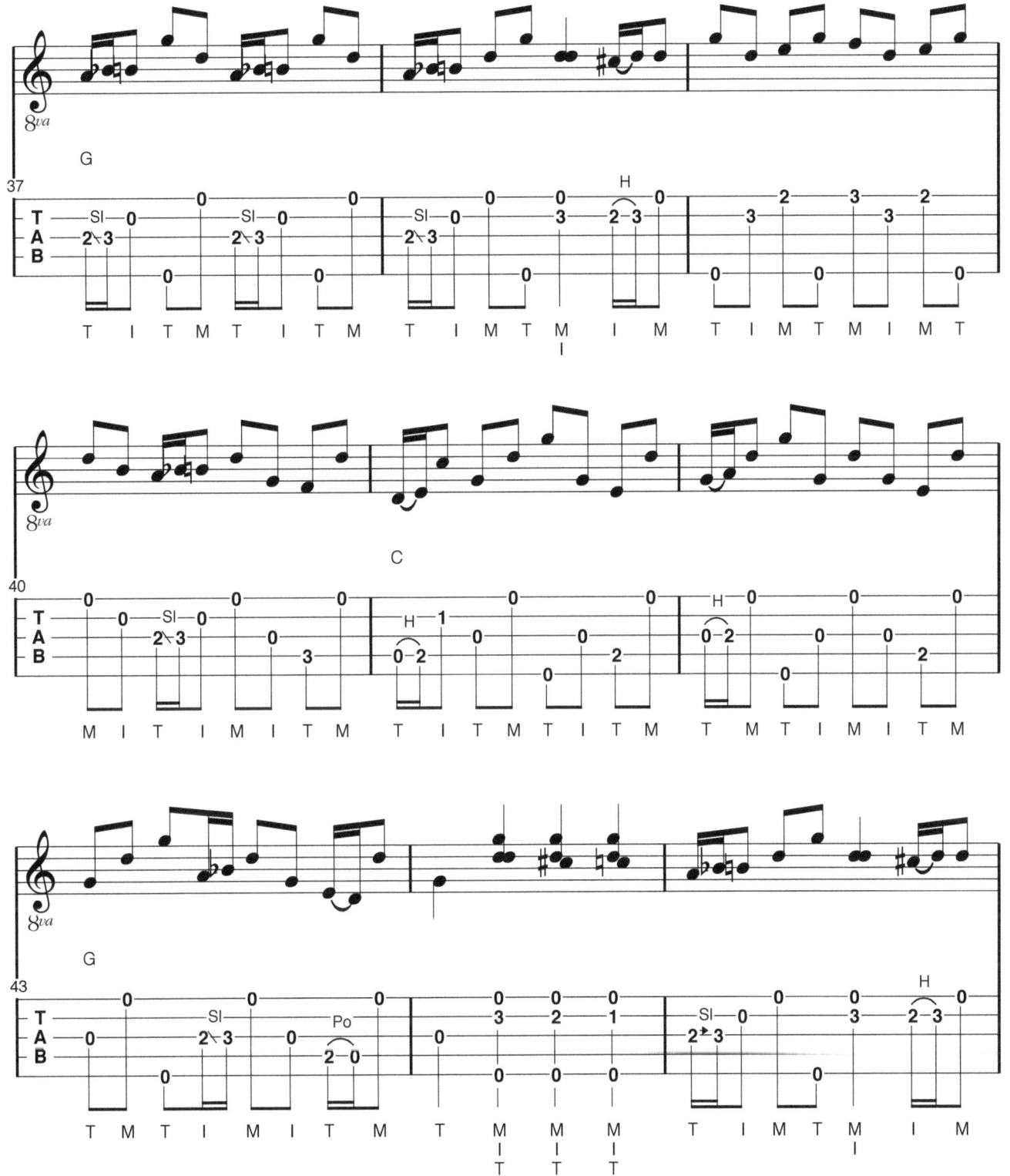

Dear Old Dixie
Page 6/12

Dear Old Dixie
Page 7/12

Dear Old Dixie
Page 8/12

61

Dear Old Dixie

Dear Old Dixie
Page 10/12

Dear Old Dixie
Page 11/12

Dear Old Dixie
Page 12/12

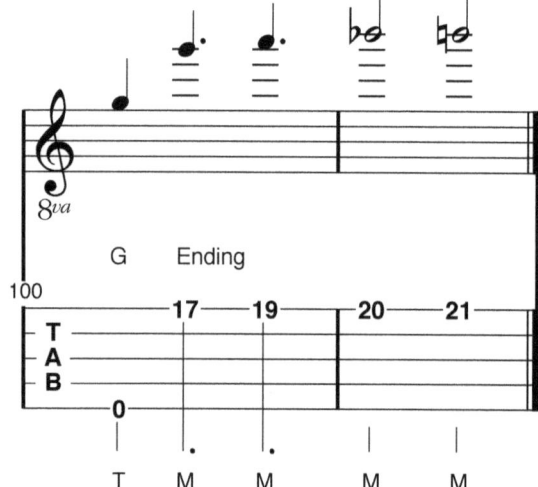

Joe and Evelyn

Key of C
Page 1/6

Joe and Evelyn
Page 2/6

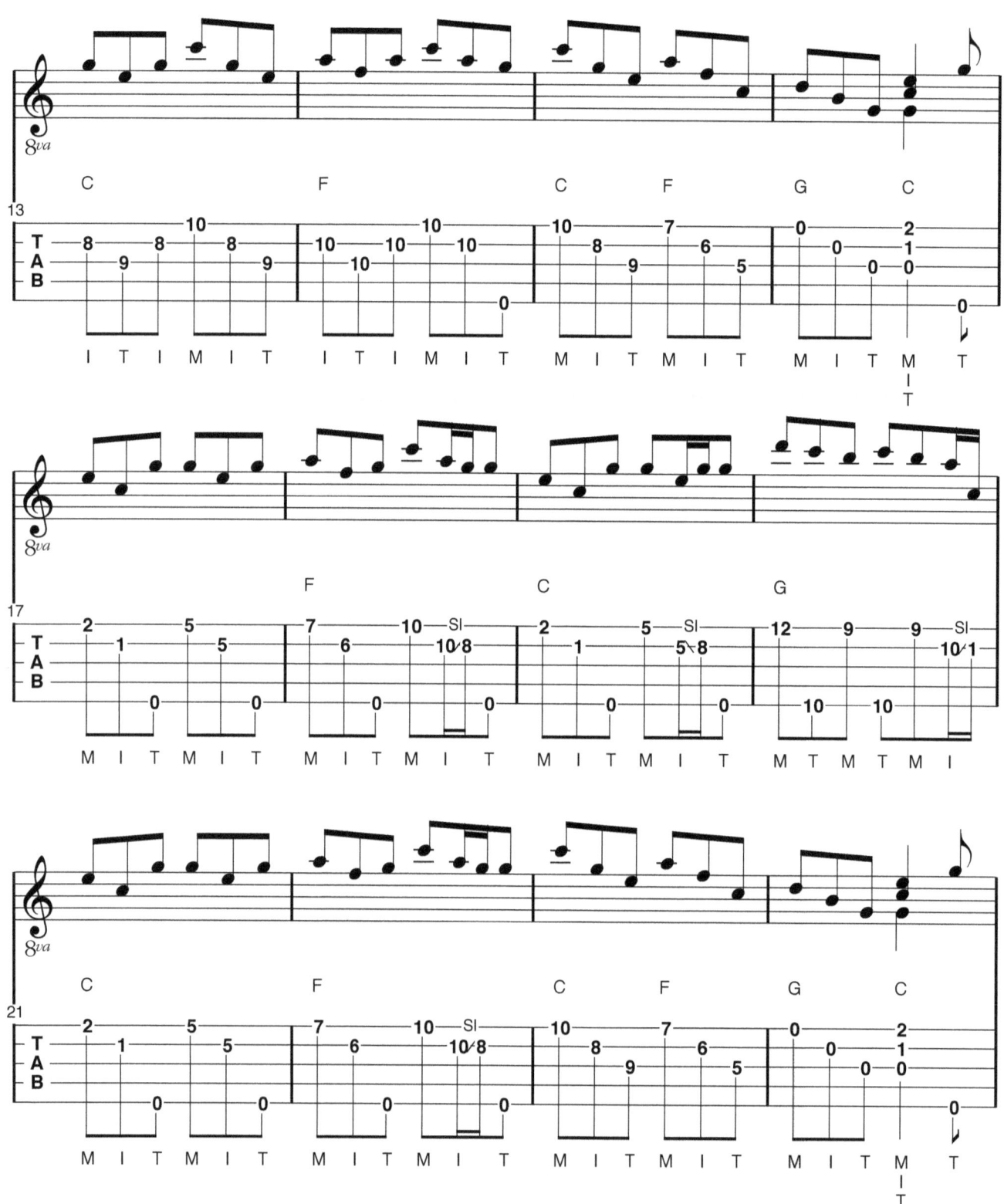

Joe and Evelyn
Page 3/6

Joe and Evelyn
Page 4/6

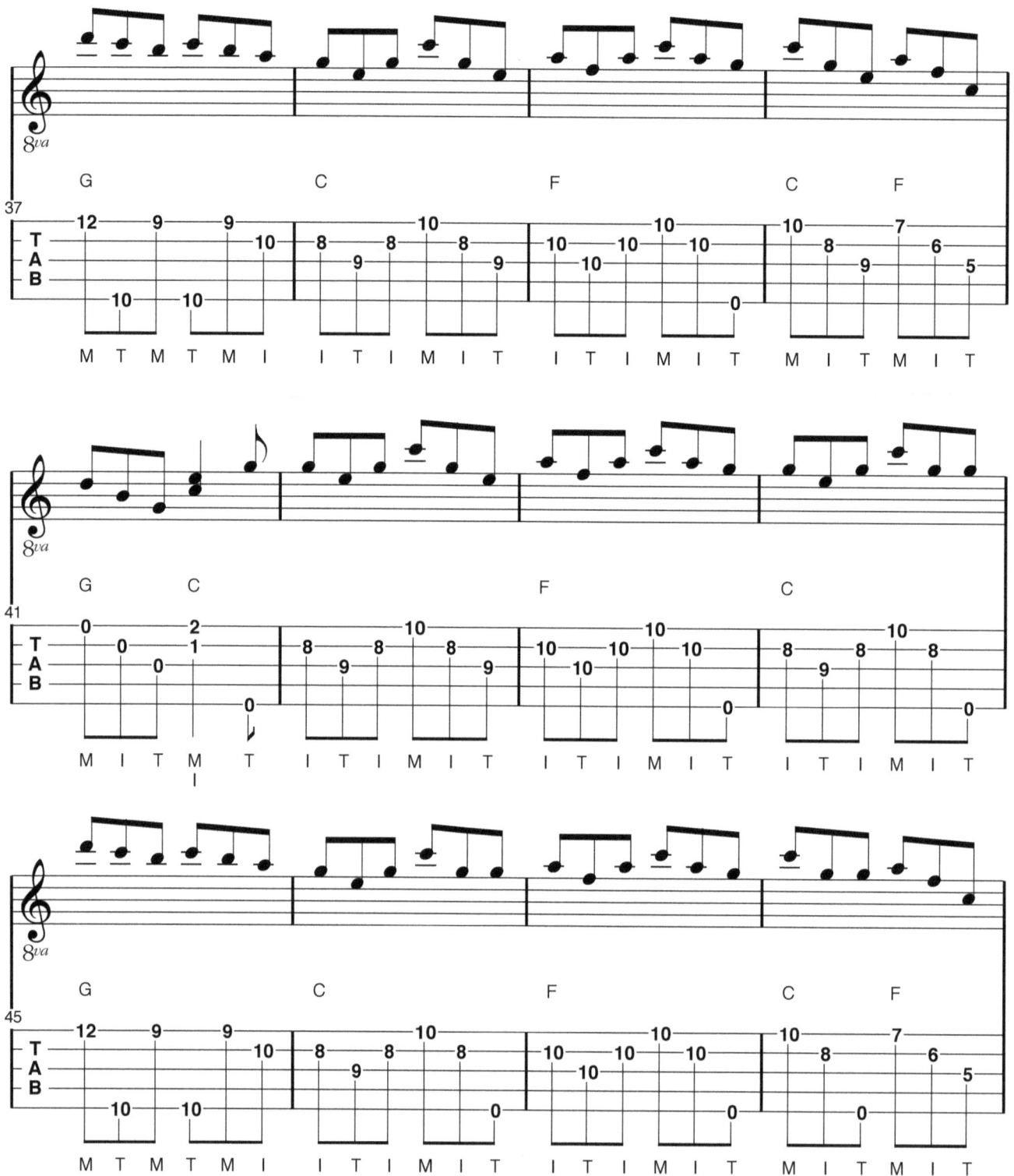

Joe and Evelyn
Page 5/6

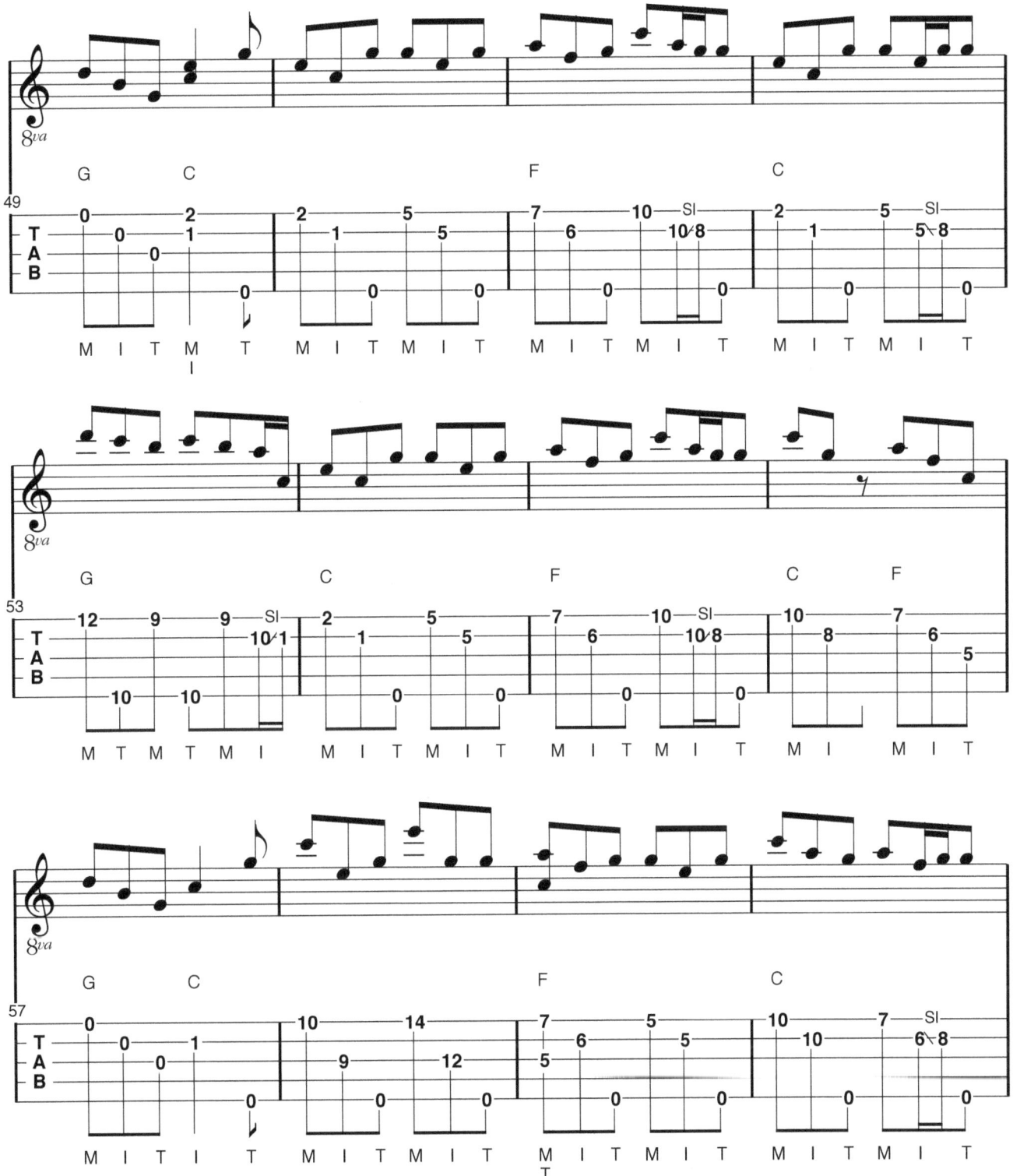

Joe and Evelyn
Page 6/6

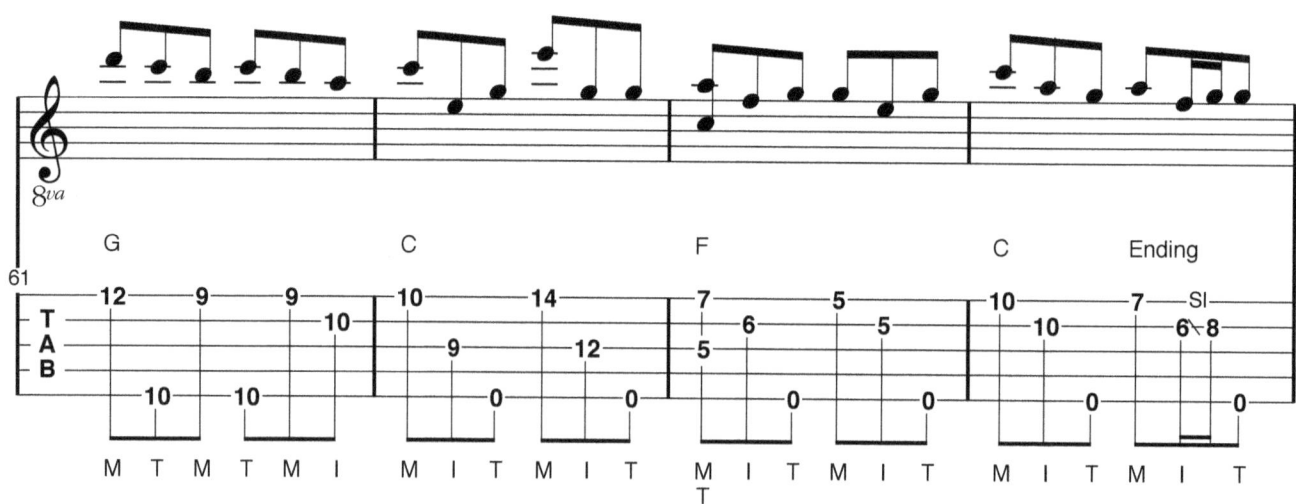

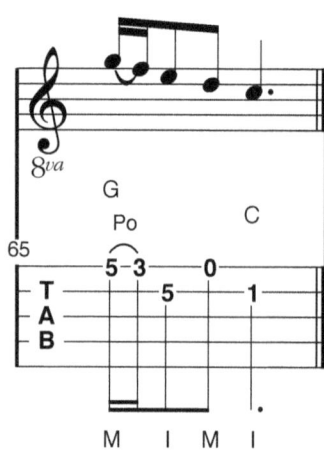

Roosters Rag

Key of G
Page 1/9

Roosters Rag
Page 2/9

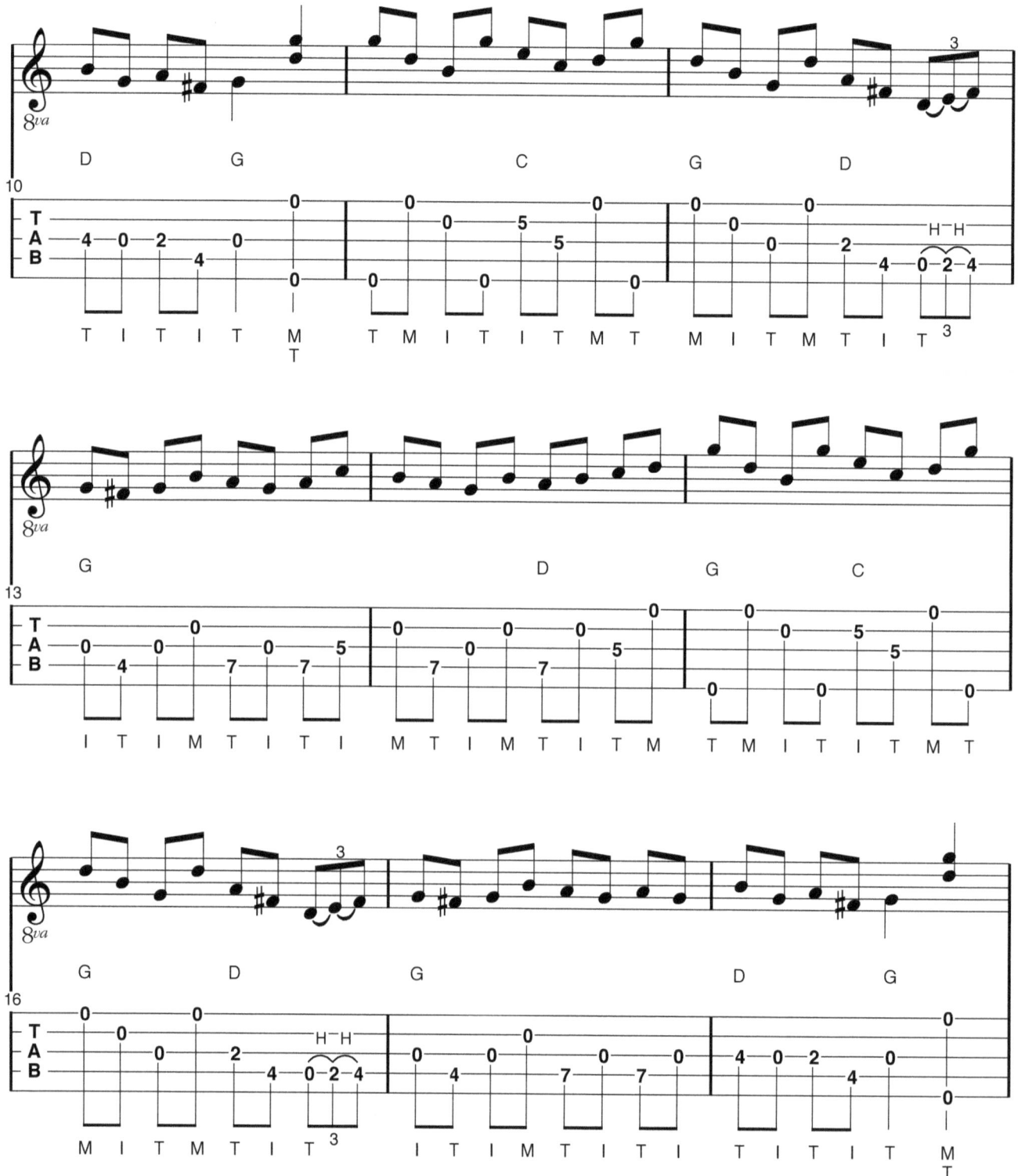

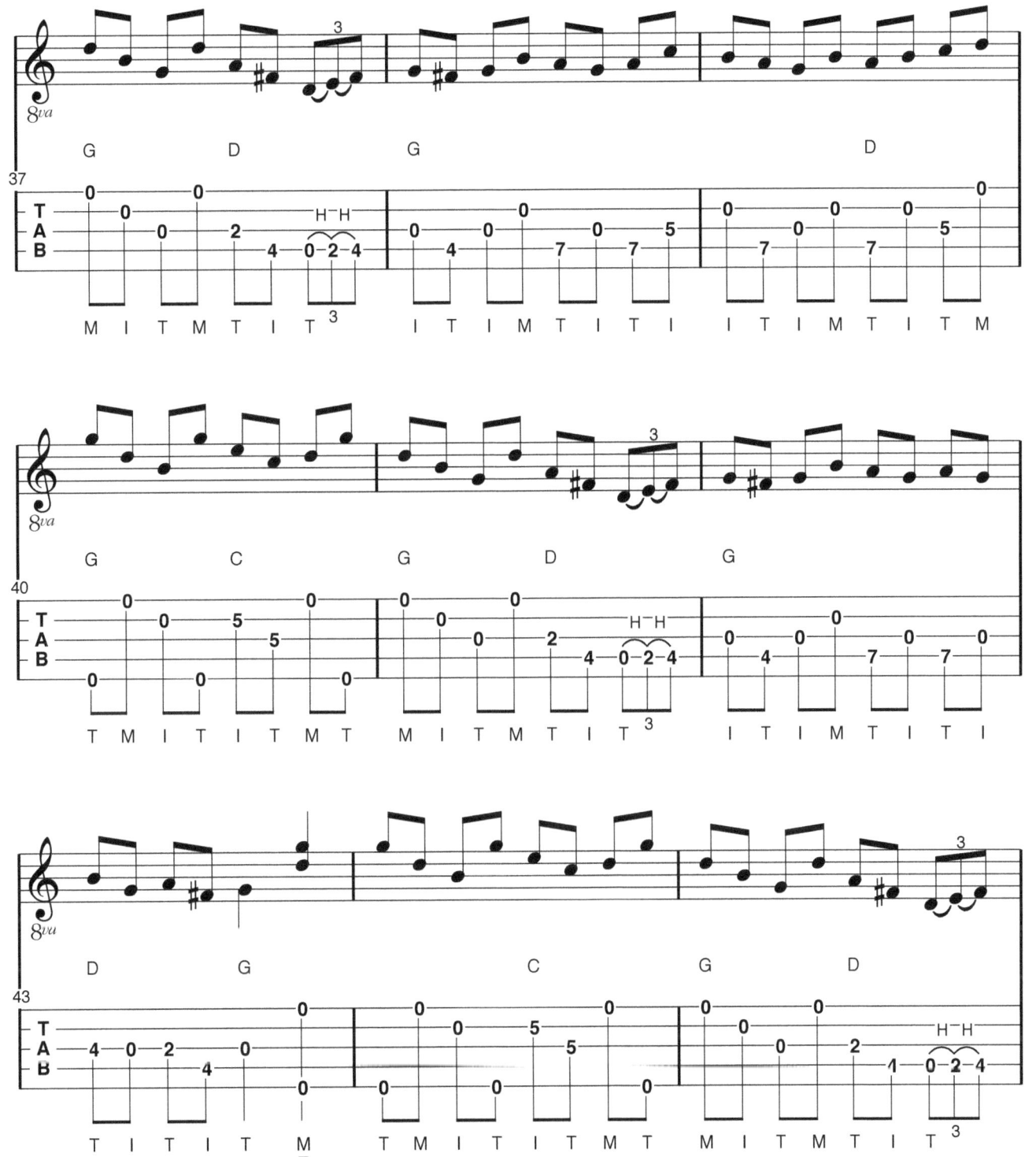

Roosters Rag
Page 6/9

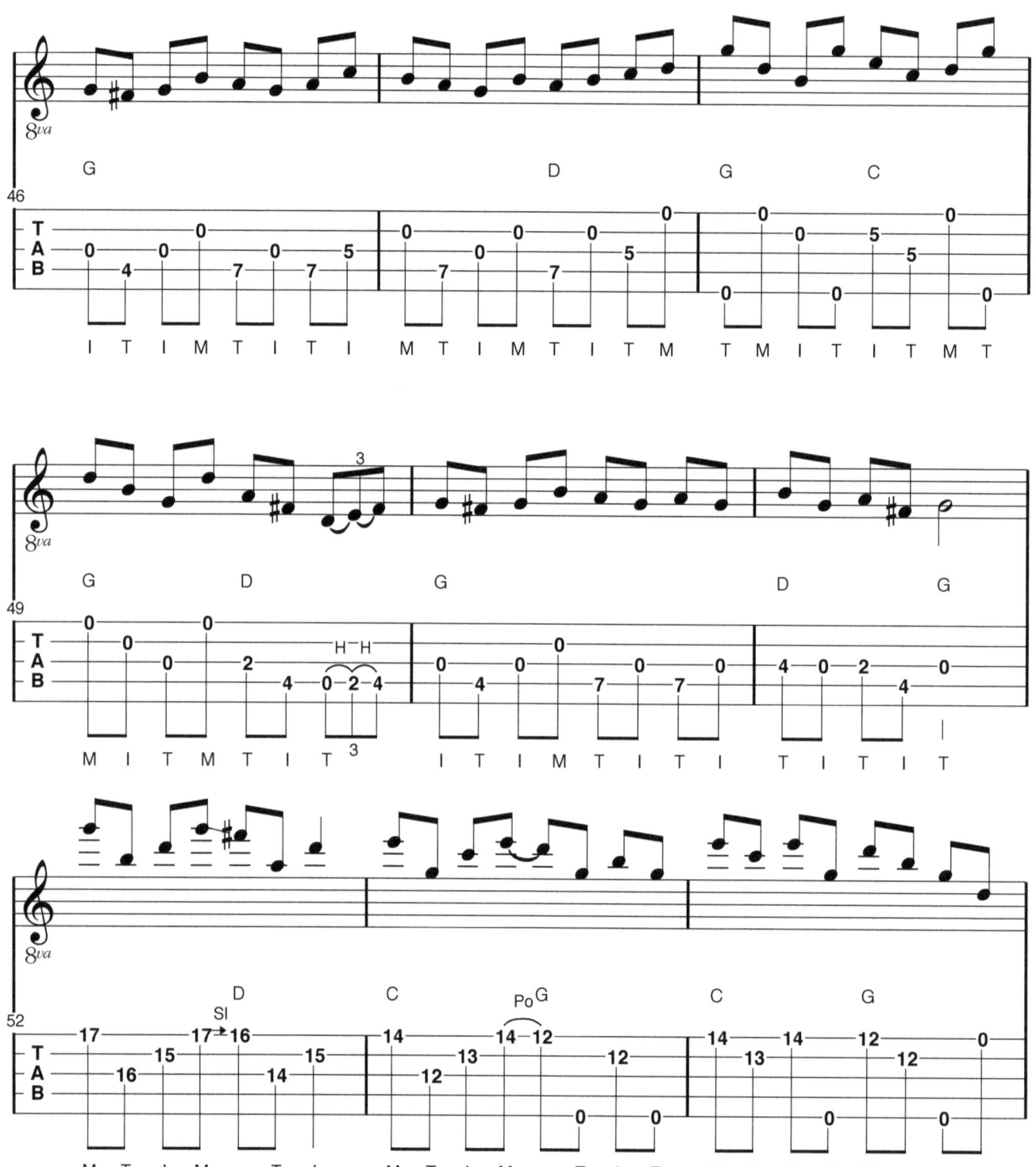

77

Roosters Rag
Page 7/9

Roosters Rag
Page 8/9

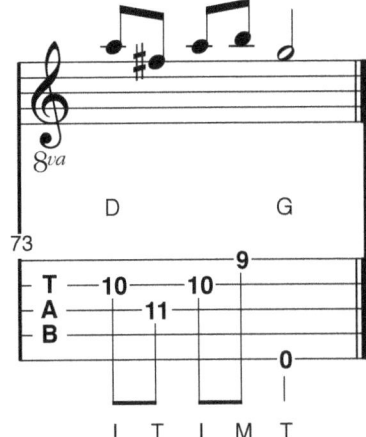

Nerissa

Key of Am, Capo 2
Page 1/4

Nerissa
Page 3/4

Nerissa
Page 4/4

Stone Bench

Key of Gm
Page 1/10

Stone Bench
Page 2/10

Stone Bench
Page 4/10

Stone Bench
Page 5/10

Stone Bench
Page 8/10

Stone Bench
Page 9/10

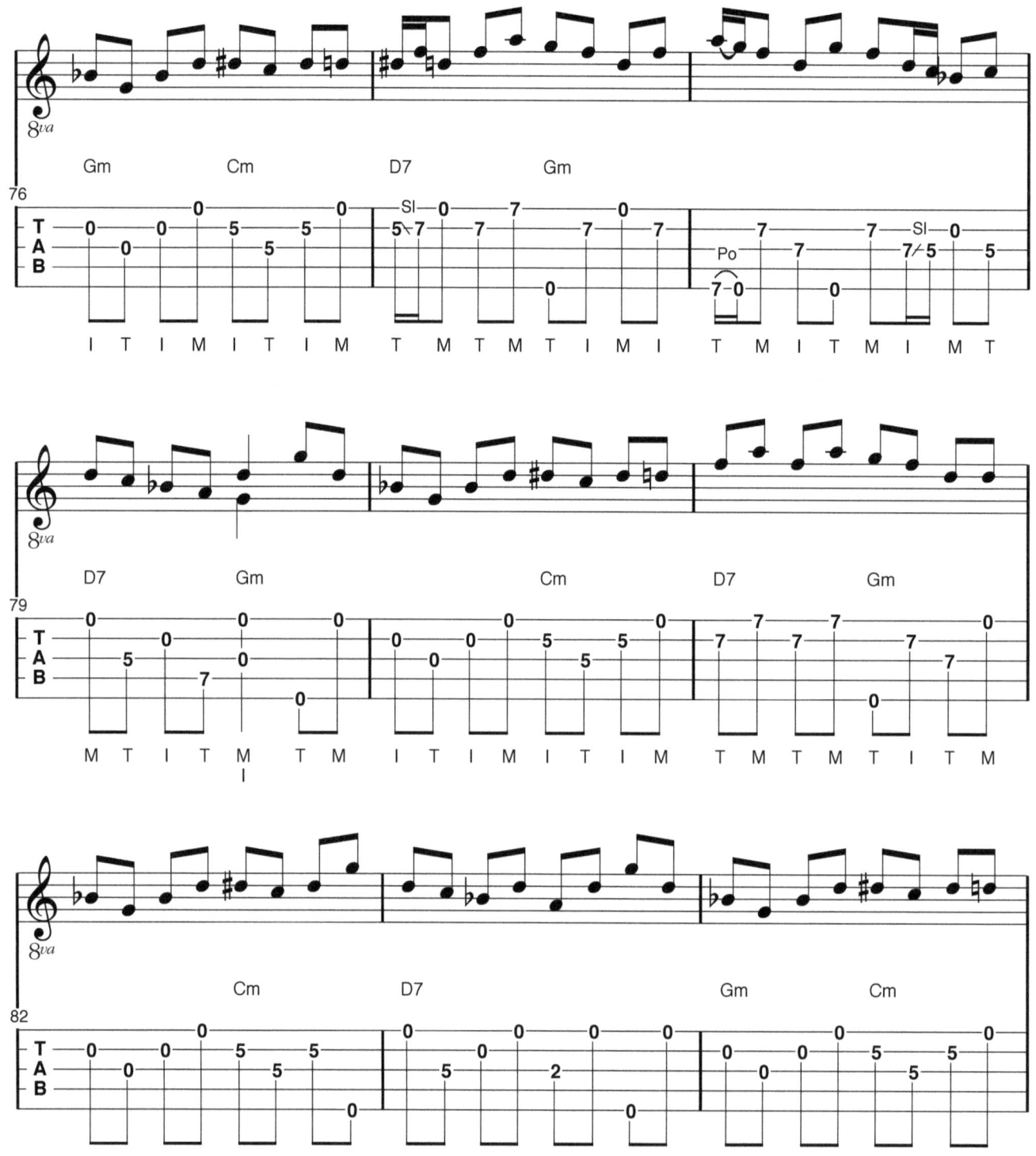

Stone Bench
Page 10/10

Discography

VISIT
danmenzone.com

CDs also available at CDBaby.com

www.ingramcontent.com/pod-product-compliance
Lightning Source LLC
Chambersburg PA
CBHW051358110526
44592CB00023B/2879